Published By:

Business in God, LLC
1901 Central Drive Suite 305
Bedford, TX 76021
Phone: 800-979-9443
ISBN – 13: 9780989505710
www.businessingod.com

Wisdom Seeds On Time Investment

Dedication

This book is dedicated to my mentor Dr. Mike Murdock. Thank you, sir, for inspiring me with your wisdom keys to start writing wisdom seeds...

A Purposeful Week Plan

"A **purposeful week** starts with a purposeful day."- Benson Agbortogo

Time, value and **relationships** are the three most important assets for generating income. Consistent profit entrepreneurs invest **time** to create **value** and use value to build **relationships**. In the future, we will elaborate on value and relationships. For now, let's focus our attention on creating "**a purposeful day**."

A purposeful day does not mean that everything will happen according to schedule. It is simply a design of how you plan to invest your time. **More importantly,** a purposeful day is a day where everything you do is motivated by love as God has instructed us.

"Do everything in love." – 1 Corinthians 16:14 NIV

There are three categories of "purposeful days" I want you to design:

1. **A purposeful Sabbath** – A day you invest more time with God in prayer and fasting. I call it; love your God day.

"If you watch your step on the Sabbath and don't use my holy day for personal advantage, if you treat the Sabbath as a day of joy, GOD's holy day as a celebration, If you honor it by refusing 'business as usual,' making money, running here and there—Then you'll be free to enjoy GOD! Oh, I'll make you ride high and soar above it all. I'll make you feast on the inheritance of your ancestor Jacob." Yes! GOD says so!" – Isaiah 58:13-14 (MSG)

2. **A Purposeful family day** – A day dedicated to taking care of yourself and your family. I call it; love yourself day.

*"If anyone wants to provide leadership in the church, good! But there are preconditions: A leader must be well-thought-of, committed to his wife, cool and collected, accessible, and hospitable. He must know what he's talking about, not be over fond of wine, not pushy but gentle, not thin-skinned, not money-hungry. He must **handle his own affairs well**, attentive to his own children and having their respect. For if someone is unable to handle his own affairs, how can he take care of God's church? He must not be a new believer, lest the position go to his head and the Devil trip him up. Outsiders must think well of him, or else the Devil will figure out a way to lure him into his trap."* – **1Timothy 3:1-7 (MSG)**

In the passage above, you can substitute Church with business or career. The key to the passage is taking care of yourself before you can take care of outside business.

3. **A purposeful work day** – A day dedicated
to serving through work. I call it; love your
customer day.

*"For you yourselves know how it is necessary to imitate
our example, for we were not disorderly or shirking of
duty when we were with you [we were not idle]. Nor did
we eat anyone's bread without paying for it, but with toil
and struggle we worked night and day, that we might not
be a burden or impose on any of you [for our support]. [It
was] not because we do not have a right [to such
support], but [we wished] to make ourselves an example
for you to follow. For while we were yet with you, we gave
you this rule and charge: If anyone will not work, neither
let him eat."* – **2 Thessalonians 3:7-10 (AMP)**

Work did not start after the fall of man in Genesis
3 as some people claim. Work was created
before the fall.

*"GOD took the Man and set him down in the
Garden of Eden to work the ground and keep it
in order."* – **Genesis 2:15 (MSG)**

In summary, the three categories of a
"purposeful day" are:

1. A purposeful sabbath day
2. A purposeful family day
3. A purposeful work day

There are also three important relationships we will use to design a purposeful day and week based on the following scripture:

*"And he answering said, thou shalt love the Lord thy God with all thy heart, and with all thy soul, and with all thy strength, and with all thy mind; and thy neighbour as thyself." – **Luke 10:27 KJV***

The three categories of relationships are:

1. Relationship with God – Love Your God
2. Relationship with yourself – Love Yourself
3. Relationship with your neighbor – Love Your Customer.

A Purposeful Day Sample Table

Relationship/Days	Sabbath	Family	Work
Your God	9 hours	3 hours	3 hours
Yourself	12 hours*	18 hours*	12 hours*
Your Customer	3 hours	3 hours	9 hours
Total	**24 hours**	**24 hours**	**24 hours**

*Note that in this example, love yourself hours include sleep time (6 -7 per day).

8

It is now time for you to design your purposeful day.

To design the purposeful day for each category, answer the following questions:

1. How many hours would you like to invest in each relationship category on your purposeful sabbath day? The total number of hours should equal 24. Write your answers in the purposeful day table below.

2. How many hours would you like to invest in each relationship category on your purposeful family day? The total number of hours should equal 24. Write your answers in the purposeful day table below.

3. How many hours would you like to invest in each relationship category on your purposeful work day? The total number of hours should equal 24. Write your answers in the purposeful day table below.

A Purposeful Day Table

Relationship/Days	Sabbath	Family	Work
Your God			
Yourself			
Your Customer			
Total			

Now that you have your purposeful day designed, let us move on to design your purposeful week.

To design your purposeful week, allocate one day to be your purposeful sabbath day, one day to be your purposeful family day and five days to be your purposeful work days.

See the example of a purposeful wee table below:

The Purposeful Week Sample Table

Days/Relationships	Your God	Yourself	Your Customer	Total Hours
Sunday	9	12	3	24
Monday	3	12	9	24
Tuesday	3	12	9	24
Wednesday	3	12	9	24
Thursday	3	12	9	24
Friday	3	12	9	24
Saturday	3	18	3	24
Grand Total	**27**	**90**	**51**	**168**

In the example above, **Sunday** is considered a purposeful Sabbath day, **Saturday** is considered a purposeful family day and **Monday – Friday** are considered the purposeful work days. Now, it is time for you to design your purposeful week following the example above.

Enter your hours in the template provided below:

Your Purposeful Week Table

Days/Relationships	Your God	Yourself	Your Customer	Total Hours
Sunday				
Monday				
Tuesday				
Wednesday				
Thursday				
Friday				
Saturday				
Grand Total				

Now that you have designed your purposeful week, you can now start investing time wisely to complete your mission and fulfil your purpose on earth.

The rest of this book will be focused on wisdom seeds. Use your calendar each day to review the previous day, view the current day and preview the following day.

Happy New Day 1

Here is today's wisdom seed:

Today Is The *Harvest* of Yesterday...And The *Seed* For Tomorrow.

How will you invest your time today?

A Purposeful Day Table Template

Relationship	Today's Investment
Your God	
Yourself	
Your Customer	
Total	**24 Hours**

Happy New Day 2

Here is today's wisdom seed:

Multitasking is like trying to poop on two toilets at the same time... No matter how skillful you are, you cannot poop on two toilets at the same time without making a mess.

How will you invest your time today?

A Purposeful Day Table Template

Relationship	Today's Investment
Your God	
Yourself	
Your Customer	
Total	**24 Hours**

Happy New Day 3

Here is today's wisdom seed:

Wealthy People Invest Time While Poor People Spend Time.

How will you invest your time today?

A Purposeful Day Table Template

Relationship	Today's Investment
Your God	
Yourself	
Your Customer	
Total	**24 Hours**

Happy New Day 4

Here is today's wisdom seed:

Inefficient Investment Of Time Is The Root Cause Of Poverty.

How will you invest your time today?

A Purposeful Day Table Template

Relationship	Today's Investment
Your God	
Yourself	
Your Customer	
Total	**24 Hours**

Happy New Day 5

Here is today's wisdom seed:

Today Is *Greater* Than Yesterday. Check Your Calendar.

How will you invest your time today?

A Purposeful Day Table Template

Relationship	Today's Investment
Your God	
Yourself	
Your Customer	
Total	**24 Hours**

Happy New Day 6

Here is today's wisdom seed:

God Is As Consistent As *Time* And *Oxygen*.

How will you invest your time today?

A Purposeful Day Table Template

Relationship	Today's Investment
Your God	
Yourself	
Your Customer	
Total	**24 Hours**

Happy New Day 7

Here is today's wisdom seed:

When You Try To Do Everything At The Same Time, You End Up Doing Nothing But When You Do One Thing At A Time, You End Up Doing Everything.

How will you invest your time today?

A Purposeful Day Table Template

Relationship	Today's Investment
Your God	
Yourself	
Your Customer	
Total	**24 Hours**

Happy New Day 8

Here is today's wisdom seed:

If You Leave Early, You Will *Never*...Be Late.

How will you invest your time today?

A Purposeful Day Table Template

Relationship	Today's Investment
Your God	
Yourself	
Your Customer	
Total	**24 Hours**

Happy New Day 9

Here is today's wisdom seed:

Those Who Plan... Are *Always* Ahead.

How will you invest your time today?

A Purposeful Day Table Template

Relationship	Today's Investment
Your God	
Yourself	
Your Customer	
Total	24 Hours

Happy New Day 10

Here is today's wisdom seed:

If You Cannot Blame Your *Watch* When *You* Are Late, You Cannot Blame *God* For Answering Your Prayers *Late*.

How will you invest your time today?

A Purposeful Day Table Template

Relationship	Today's Investment
Your God	
Yourself	
Your Customer	
Total	**24 Hours**

Happy New Day 11

Here is today's wisdom seed:

The Successful Invest Time In A Few Things... While The Unsuccessful Spread Themselves Thin.

How will you invest your time today?

A Purposeful Day Table Template

Relationship	Today's Investment
Your God	
Yourself	
Your Customer	
Total	**24 Hours**

Happy New Day 12

Here is today's wisdom seed:

Wealthy People Use Calendars To Plan While Poor People Use Their Heads To Plan.

How will you invest your time today?

A Purposeful Day Table Template

Relationship	Today's Investment
Your God	
Yourself	
Your Customer	
Total	**24 Hours**

Happy New Day 13

Here is today's wisdom seed:

Without An *Appointment*, You Cannot Be Late.

How will you invest your time today?

A Purposeful Day Table Template

Relationship	Today's Investment
Your God	
Yourself	
Your Customer	
Total	24 Hours

Happy New Day 14

Here is today's wisdom seed:

God's Time...Is *Now*.

How will you invest your time today?

A Purposeful Day Table Template

Relationship	Today's Investment
Your God	
Yourself	
Your Customer	
Total	**24 Hours**

Happy New Day 15

Here is today's wisdom seed:

There Is Time...
For *Everything*.

How will you invest your time today?

A Purposeful Day Table Template

Relationship	Today's Investment
Your God	
Yourself	
Your Customer	
Total	**24 Hours**

Happy New Day 16

Here is today's wisdom seed:

Your Time Management Is A Clue To Your Money Management.

How will you invest your time today?

A Purposeful Day Table Template

Relationship	Today's Investment
Your God	
Yourself	
Your Customer	
Total	**24 Hours**

Happy New Day 17

Here is today's wisdom seed:

When You Do The Right *Thing* At The Right Time, You Will *Always* Be Right.

How will you invest your time today?

A Purposeful Day Table Template

Relationship	Today's Investment
Your God	
Yourself	
Your Customer	
Total	**24 Hours**

Happy New Day 18

Here is today's wisdom seed:

Your Calendar Empowers You To Preview The Past, View The Present And Preview The Future.

How will you invest your time today?

A Purposeful Day Table Template

Relationship	Today's Investment
Your God	
Yourself	
Your Customer	
Total	**24 Hours**

Happy New Day 19

Here is today's wisdom seed:

Every Seed Has An *Expected* Time To Produce A Harvest.

How will you invest your time today?

A Purposeful Day Table Template

Relationship	Today's Investment
Your God	
Yourself	
Your Customer	
Total	24 Hours

Happy New Day 20

Here is today's wisdom seed:

Your Calendar Is The *Evidence*...Of Your *Love*.

How will you invest your time today?

A Purposeful Day Table Template

Relationship	Today's Investment
Your God	
Yourself	
Your Customer	
Total	**24 Hours**

Happy New Day 21

Here is today's wisdom seed:

The Highest *Return* On Time...Is Time *Invested* In God's Presence.

How will you invest your time today?

A Purposeful Day Table Template

Relationship	Today's Investment
Your God	
Yourself	
Your Customer	
Total	**24 Hours**

Happy New Day 22

Here is today's wisdom seed:

If You Do Not Invest Time To Plan, You Will Waste More Time In Confusion.

How will you invest your time today?

A Purposeful Day Table Template

Relationship	Today's Investment
Your God	
Yourself	
Your Customer	
Total	24 Hours

Happy New Day 23

Here is today's wisdom seed:

A Full-Time Worker... Is A Worker Who Works Wholeheartedly.

How will you invest your time today?

A Purposeful Day Table Template

Relationship	Today's Investment
Your God	
Yourself	
Your Customer	
Total	**24 Hours**

Happy New Day 24

Here is today's wisdom seed:

Today Is An Opportunity... To Bury Yesterday And Birth Tomorrow.

How will you invest your time today?

A Purposeful Day Table Template

Relationship	Today's Investment
Your God	
Yourself	
Your Customer	
Total	**24 Hours**

Happy New Day 25

Here is today's wisdom seed:

Whatever *Kills*, *Steals* Or *Destroys* Your Time... Is *Demonic*.

How will you invest your time today?

A Purposeful Day Table Template

Relationship	Today's Investment
Your God	
Yourself	
Your Customer	
Total	**24 Hours**

Happy New Day 26

Here is today's wisdom seed:

Tracking Time Enables You To Identify... Divine *Direction* And Demonic *Distractions*.

How will you invest your time today?

A Purposeful Day Table Template

Relationship	Today's Investment
Your God	
Yourself	
Your Customer	
Total	**24 Hours**

Happy New Day 27

Here is today's wisdom seed:

Time Does Not *Discriminate* Against Age, Color, Gender, Nationality Or Education Level.

How will you invest your time today?

A Purposeful Day Table Template

Relationship	Today's Investment
Your God	
Yourself	
Your Customer	
Total	**24 Hours**

Happy New Day 28

Here is today's wisdom seed:

24 Hours Is *Enough...* To Fulfill Your Purpose Each Day.

How will you invest your time today?

A Purposeful Day Table Template

Relationship	Today's Investment
Your God	
Yourself	
Your Customer	
Total	**24 Hours**

Happy New Day 29

Here is today's wisdom seed:

A New Year...
Is A *Combination*
Of 365 *New Days.*

How will you invest your time today?

A Purposeful Day Table Template

Relationship	Today's Investment
Your God	
Yourself	
Your Customer	
Total	**24 Hours**

Happy New Day 30

Here is today's wisdom seed:

Time Is Like *Soil*.
Whatever You *Plant*...
It Will *Grow*.

How will you invest your time today?

A Purposeful Day Table Template

Relationship	Today's Investment
Your God	
Yourself	
Your Customer	
Total	**24 Hours**

Happy New Day 31

Here is today's wisdom seed:

When You *Start* At The End, You *Finish* Before You Start.

How will you invest your time today?

A Purposeful Day Table Template

Relationship	Today's Investment
Your God	
Yourself	
Your Customer	
Total	24 Hours

Daily Wisdom Seeds

In this book, I have 31 wisdom seeds with you since there are 31 days in the longest month.

Would you like to receive more wisdom seeds directly to your phone daily?

Take the following steps:

Step 1:

Simply text the word **"Time"** to **817- 591- 7486.**

Step 2:

Check your phone and follow the directions in the text message you received.

Step 3:

Start receiving daily wisdom seeds from us.

Other Books

These are other books you can order from our bookstore at:

www.businessingod.com/books

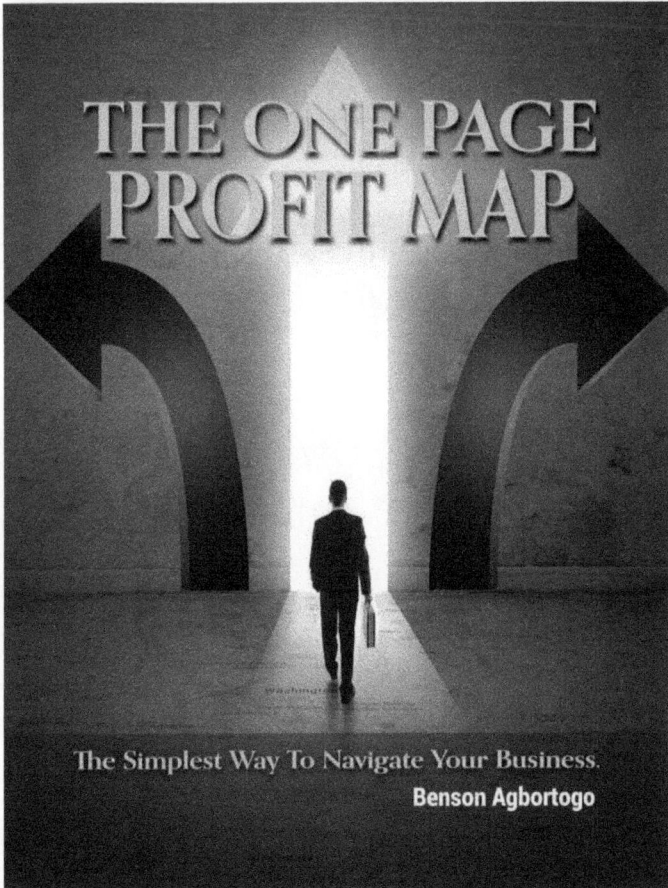

www.ingramcontent.com/pod-product-compliance
Lightning Source LLC
Chambersburg PA
CBHW022056190326
41520CB00008B/789